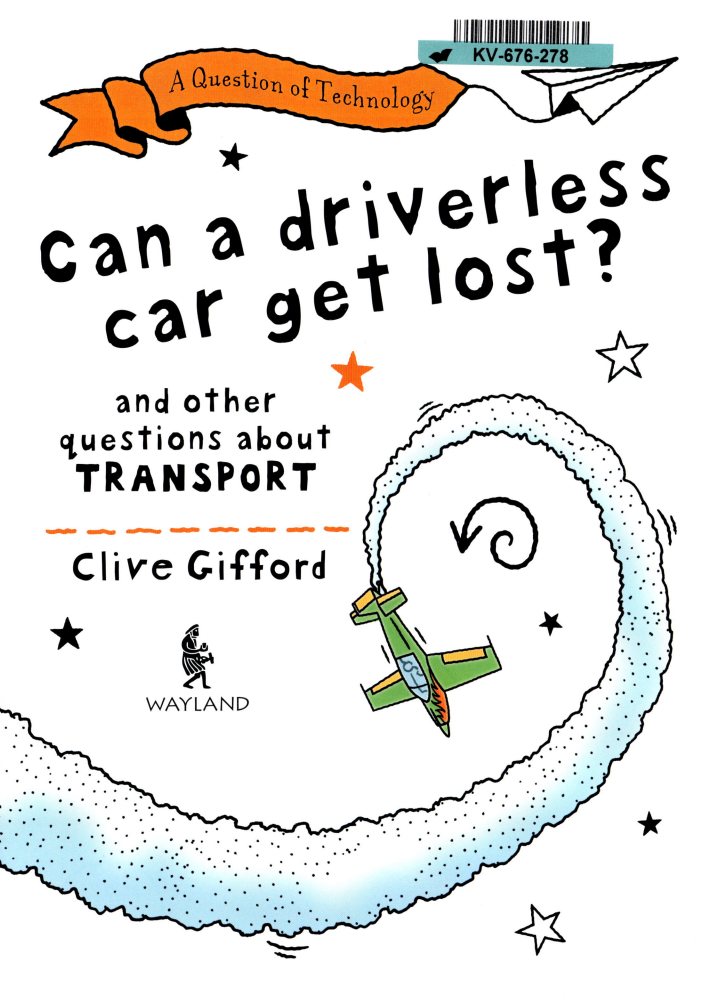

A Question of Technology

Can a driverless car get lost?

and other questions about TRANSPORT

Clive Gifford

WAYLAND

First published in Great Britain in 2022
by Wayland

Credits:
Editors: Julia Bird; Julia Adams
Design and illustrations: Matt Lilly
Cover design: Matt Lilly

HB ISBN 978 1 5263 1994 4
PB ISBN 978 1 5263 1995 1

Printed and bound in China

MIX
Paper from
responsible sources
FSC® C104740

Picture credits:

Alamy: Jim West cover, 7tr.
Getty Images: Larry Mayer 9tl; Icon Sportswire 25b.
Matt Lilly: 20t.
NASA: 5tr.
Shutterstock: Wirestock Creators 10–11b;
Ahmed Faizal Yahya 15t; Christopher Lyzcen 15c;
Beniost 18c; Elmar Gubish 19t; Soos Jozef 21c;
Roi Shomer 21b; mastersky 23br; Hasrullnizam 25t;
Kemdim 26t; Noreismail 27t.

Wayland
An imprint of
Hachette Children's Group
Part of Hodder and Stoughton
Carmelite House
50 Victoria Embankment
London EC4Y 0DZ

An Hachette UK Company
www.hachette.co.uk
www.hachettechildrens.co.uk

Contents

Transport tech

Transport is all about the machines that help make travel faster, easier and safer. Where would you be without a bus into town or a lift in a car? And what about flying to your holiday abroad ...?

And it's not just people ...

More than 90 per cent of all the goods you buy – from pineapples to pairs of jeans – have travelled by sea, mostly on giant container ships that criss-cross the globe.

ER, WHICH CONTAINER DID YOU LEAVE THE KEYS IN?

Power sources

Transport connects and powers the modern world, but it wasn't always this way. Wheels were invented around 5,000 years ago, but the only way of turning them for 4,800 years was animal power.

The invention of first steam, and then internal combustion engines, (see pages 22–23), revolutionised transport.

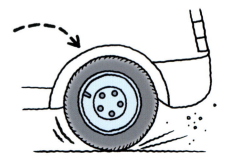

Dozens of engineers and pioneers have since helped to make modern transport possible.

The Wright brothers, Orville and Wilbur, were US bicycle repairers fascinated with flight. In 1903, they flew the first heavier-than-air aircraft.

Karl Benz built the first practical motor vehicle in 1885. His wife, Bertha, used it to make the first epic road trip – a 170km-long journey around Germany!

I LAY ON MY STOMACH AND PULLED WIRES TO STEER THE PLANE.

On the move

Transport is pretty amazing and here are some mind-blowing facts to prove it.

Some trains are more than 3 km long!

There are more than 1.4 billion vehicles on the world's roads.

On 25 July 2019, there were over 230,000 aircraft flights made – the busiest day in aviation history.

There are 4 million more bicycles in the Netherlands than there are people.

Can a driverless car get lost?

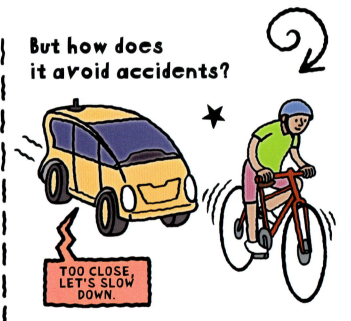

Not unless it tries really hard!

Like human drivers, a driverless car uses satnavs to follow a route. It follows these instructions from orbiting satellites and won't change course unless there is a hazard ahead.

YOU ARE HERE!

I'm in charge

A driverless car's controller is a computer. Think of it as the car's boss. It's also a real busybody, constantly gathering information about the car's position, speed and direction.

MUST UPDATE SOFTWARE – NO ZEBRA CROSSING HERE!

It can then plot the vehicle's next move and send signals to electric motors which change and control the car's speed, braking and steering.
Ingenious!

But how does it avoid accidents?

TOO CLOSE, LET'S SLOW DOWN.

The car relies on lots of sensors as its eyes and ears. Many, like RADAR and ultrasonic sensors, bounce invisible energy waves off objects to work out how close they are to the car. Others can identify traffic signs or track the speed of other vehicles.

Sensor-ational

A LiDAR turret spins and uses invisible laser beams to build up a 3D map of the car's surroundings.

Between 8 and 40 cameras all over the car identify kerb edges, traffic signs, lights and unexpected obstacles.

Ultrasonic sensors bounce sound off nearby objects to measure short distances accurately. They're especially useful during parking.

Infrared sensors* spot lane markings, pedestrians and cyclists close by.

RADAR measures distances and changes in speed of vehicles in front and behind.

*These sensors send back masses of information to the controller many times every second.

Working together

The sensors' zones overlap so parts of the road are checked on by more than one device. When moving a two-tonne car around busy roads, it's no bad thing to have a second opinion!

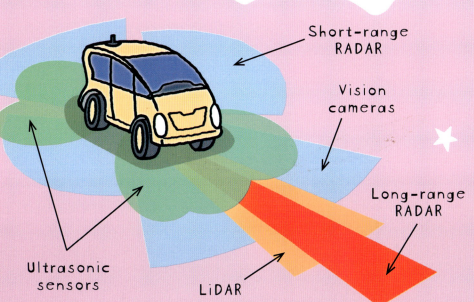

Short-range RADAR

Vision cameras

Long-range RADAR

Ultrasonic sensors

LiDAR

How does a plane turn left?

On the ground, big planes are steered using nose wheels which the pilot can turn left or right using a lever inside the cockpit. Up in the air, though, it's a different matter.

In control

When flying, planes rely on large, hinged flaps or panels on their wings and tails to change direction.

THESE ARE CALLED CONTROL SURFACES.

When moved, they deflect some of the air flowing round the plane, which changes the plane's direction.

Rudder

Elevators

Aileron

Pitch-yaw-roll

A flying plane can change its course by moving in one of three directions...

Elevators alter the **pitch**. Pitch is when the nose points up or down. The plane either climbs or dives as a result.

Ailerons create **roll**. Roll is when one wing dips down and the other travels upwards. This is also called 'banking'.

Rudder creates **yaw**. Yaw is when the nose of the plane turns to the left or the right.

Cockpit controls

In the cockpit of a small aircraft, the pilot steers using a pair of foot pedals called a rudder bar and a joystick or control column. These move the control surfaces by pulling cables or by sending radio signals to small motors.

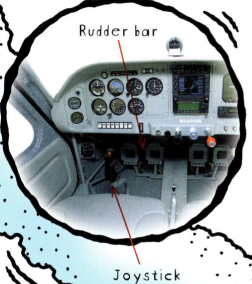

Rudder bar

Joystick

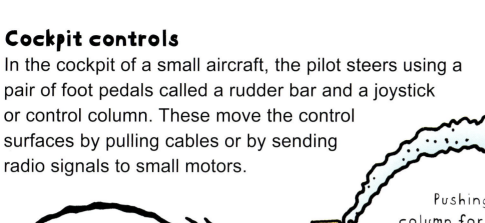

Pushing the column forward, for example, causes the plane's nose to point down. Pulling it back points the nose up and causes the plane to climb.

WHOAAH!!

But back to our original question!

What about turning left?

To turn left, the pilot moves the control column leftwards.

This moves the left wing's aileron up and the right wing's aileron down. The left wing travels down and the right wing travels up. The pilot also turns the rudder to the right. This points the plane's nose to the left. The plane can now make a smooth, banked turn to the left.

... AND LEFT!

Why doesn't a 200,000-tonne ship sink?

Plip!

Plip!

Plop!

When you skim a pebble across a lake or sea, it may skip a few times before sinking. Yet, a large cruise or cargo ship floats despite weighing hundreds of thousands of times more.

How is that possible?

A bit dense

Your pebble's problem is that it's too dense. That means it has a lot of matter stuffed inside it for its size. If an object is denser than water, it sinks. If something is less dense than water, such as a piece of wood or an air-filled lilo, it floats.

But a ship must be heavier than a lilo?

Definitely! The *Harmony of the Seas* (below) cruise ship, for example, weighs a monumental **226,963** tonnes, or, to put another way, about as much as **37,800** elephants.

362 m long
70 m tall
66 m wide

OOF! THAT'S HEAVY!

Royal Caribbean INTERNATIONAL

But the ship's giant hull contains **HUGE** amounts of air which is far less dense than water. As a result, the whole ship is less dense than water and floats.

The naked truth

Archimedes was a super-smart ancient Greek scientist born 2,300 years ago. He figured out precisely why things float. When an object is put in water it displaces (pushes away) some water which, in turn, pushes back against the object.

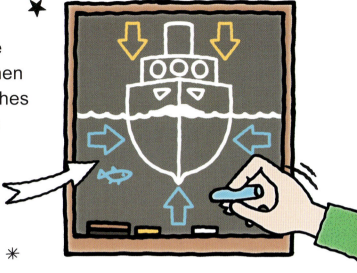

If the object is less dense than water, the force of the water pushing back is enough to keep it afloat.

HE'S OFF AGAIN!

At the time Archimedes discovered this, he was having a bath. He was so delighted he is said to have jumped out of the water, and ran down the street naked, yelling, **'EUREKA!'** (meaning, 'I've found it!' in Greek).

Back to the question

Because of their great size, big ships push away **A LOT** of water to make room for themselves. The amount of force pushing back on them from the water is also huge.

So, ships float because they weigh less than the weight of the water they push away. **Simple!**

How do gears make my bike super speedy?

To be honest, it's all up to you and your pedal power. Gears, though, can help you build speed and make it easier when travelling up or downhill.

WHOOOAHHH!

May the force be with you

Bike gears are toothed wheels which alter a force in some way. Some allow force to be transferred to a different place, such as the chain wheel attached to your pedals.

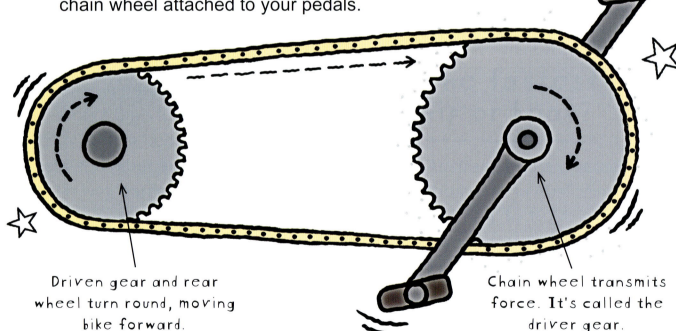

Driven gear and rear wheel turn round, moving bike forward.

Chain wheel transmits force. It's called the driver gear.

When you start pedalling, the chain wheel turns and, with a little help from your bike chain, transmits force to the gear on the back wheel. This gear turns the rear wheel round and moves your bike forward.

So, how do I go faster?

The difference in size between your chain wheel and the driven gear at the rear is called a gear ratio. If you increase the ratio by choosing a smaller driven gear, then the gear and rear wheel turn faster.

A **4:1** gear ratio means that for every complete turn of the pedals, your rear wheel makes four complete turns. You'd be flying!

What's the catch?

The extra speed comes at a cost – you have to put in much more effort when using a high gear ratio. Having different gears means you can change the force depending on the circumstances. So, when you're tired or cycling up a steep slope, you may opt for a much lower gear ratio.

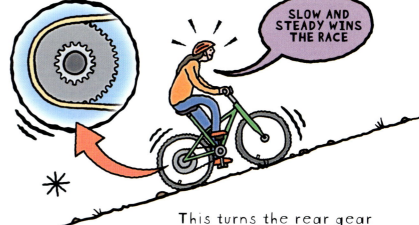

WHEEEE!

SLOW AND STEADY WINS THE RACE

This turns the rear gear and back wheel more slowly so you don't travel as far for each turn of the pedals. But it requires less force so it's easier to keep pedalling.

What, no gears?

Early bikes had no gears.

The pedals were attached directly to the front wheel so one turn of the pedals equalled one turn of the wheel. The only way to build a faster bike without gears was to make the front wheel bigger... and bigger!

This resulted in penny-farthing bicycles with front wheels bigger than you are tall. With the saddle almost 2 m off the ground, these bikes were hard to get on and off, but very easy to crash or topple over!

WISH I'D BOUGHT A BMX INSTEAD!

Penny-farthing

Could an F1 car drive upside-down on a ceiling?

PHEW, THAT WAS CLOSE!

Yes. In theory.

Formula One (F1) cars are incredible high-performance machines. They can accelerate from 0 to 100 km/h in 2.6 seconds, power in and out of tight corners at speed and race at over 320 km/h.

Get a grip

A big part of their high performance is the great grip these cars get on the track. And a lot of that is down to how they direct air around their bodies. This is why F1 car designers spend thousands of hours testing and perfecting car body and wing shapes.

Cars with wings?

You heard it correctly. F1 cars have a large front wing (and a big rear one as well). Where aircraft wings create lift, the car's wings work the other way round. They create low air pressure underneath the car to produce negative lift, better known as **DOWNFORCE**.

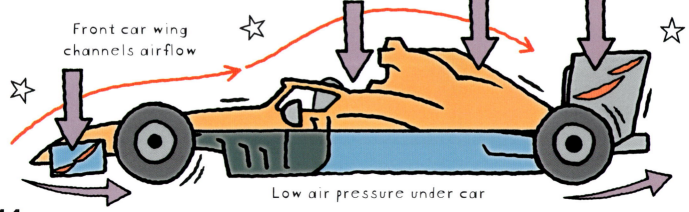

The car's wings and body all help create downforce.

Downforce presses car down

Front car wing channels airflow

Low air pressure under car

Gripping stuff

Downforce helps the car's tyres grip the track and move the car forwards as they spin. It allows the driver to make tight turns and accelerate away at high speed without the car's wheels flying up off the track.

WHOAH! NOT ENOUGH DOWNFORCE!

Downforce double

The faster the airflow, the more downforce the car can create – as much as three or four times the weight of the car. So, at speeds above 200 km/h the downforce would be enough to keep the car gripping the ceiling of a tunnel. Getting the car up on the ceiling at a fast enough speed in the first place is quite another question though!

Why do my ears pop when I'm flying?

It's all about air and pressure. Air high in the Earth's atmosphere pushes down on the air below it which, in turn, pushes down on the Earth's surface. The force of the air at ground level is called atmospheric pressure.

As you rise higher, the pressure decreases. At 5,500 m, air pressure is half of what it is at sea level.

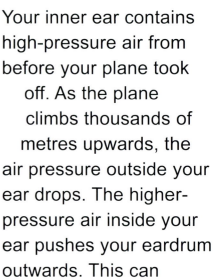

OWW!

Ear air

Apart from being a neat tongue-twister (try saying it 10 times, fast), ear air is the cause of ear pain and pops when you fly.

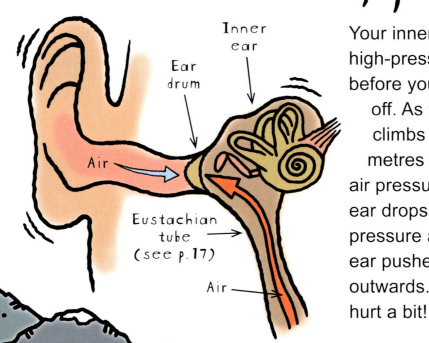

Inner ear

Ear drum

Air

Eustachian tube (see p.17)

Air

Your inner ear contains high-pressure air from before your plane took off. As the plane climbs thousands of metres upwards, the air pressure outside your ear drops. The higher-pressure air inside your ear pushes your eardrum outwards. This can hurt a bit!

Sea level

POP!

Your body tries to balance the pressure out. It does this by releasing air from your ears out into your throat through a small channel called the Eustachian tube. The opening of these tubes, after you chew gum or waggle your jaw, is the popping sound you feel.

Why do planes fly so high?

Passenger airliners cruise at altitudes of 10,600 m or more. It seems a lot of effort and fuel to get the plane to climb that high, so why do they do it?

For two reasons

① Almost all of Earth's weather occurs below this altitude. This means planes up high encounter fewer storms and turbulence, and less use of airline sick bags!

② Because air at high altitudes is less dense, planes come up against far less resistance from it. (This resistance is better known as drag.) Less drag means planes don't have to work so hard to fly at their ideal speed, so they consume a lot less fuel.

THIS IS YOUR CAPTAIN SPEAKING. SORRY FOR THE TURBULENCE.

I KNEW WE SHOULDN'T HAVE FLOWN WITH LOW-ALTITUDE AIRWAYS!

Are crash test dummies actually really smart?

Crash test dummies are put through 100 or more vehicle crashes every year. They may be lifeless but they're crammed full of smart technology.

I THINK NEXT TIME, I'LL TAKE THE BUS!

Crash!

Many dummies contain more than 200 sensors.

Model employees

Crash test dummies are model humans, put to work by car makers and road safety organisations to mimic the injuries people might suffer in accidents. Modern dummies are **PACKED** full of electronic sensors to register all the effects of a major crash or impact.

Dummy data

The sensors record changing forces and speeds hundreds of times a second. Each dummy might collect **30,000** or more pieces of data from its sensors during a crash lasting less than one second.

This data is analysed in order to understand forces and impacts better and design and build safer vehicles.

Neck and spine bend just like a person's. Sensors inside work out what injury might be caused by a particular type of impact.

Sensors record how the arms and legs move during impact.

Accelerometers help gauge how fast part of the dummy is flung during impact.

The amount of force striking parts of the dummy are measured by devices called load cells.

Potentiometers measure how much joints twist in a crash.

Meet the family

Different size and weight dummies are produced to represent typical members of the human population, from toddlers and schoolchildren to big adults.

ARE WE THERE YET?

How do helicopters stay up?

Ever watched a heavy helicopter just hang in mid-air? How does it manage to hover when, unlike other aircraft, it lacks wings to give it lift?

THERE GOES OUR LUNCH!

Hovering is great for rescuing people trapped at sea or on land in a natural disaster.

The simple answer is that it **DOES** have wings. Sort of. Each of its long, thin rotor blades have an aerofoil shape, just like a plane's wing.

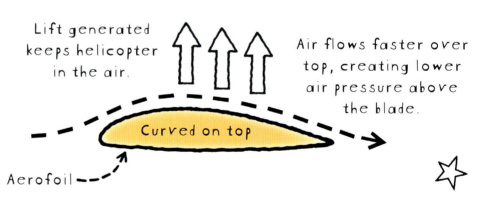

Lift generated keeps helicopter in the air.

Air flows faster over top, creating lower air pressure above the blade.

Curved on top

Aerofoil

A plane gains lift by flying forwards fast. This results in lots of air flowing over its wings, generating lift. A helicopter gets its airflow even when hovering still in the sky. It does this by using motors to spin its rotor blades quickly through the air.

 **How quickly?** Up to 500 complete spins a minute. That's fast!

Torque talk

When a moving force (called the action) occurs, a force equally big occurs in the opposite direction (called the reaction). The spinning rotor blades create an action called torque. The natural reaction to torque is for the helicopter's body to spin in the opposite direction.

Dizzy pilots and uncontrollable helicopters would result if smart engineers hadn't found two main ways of tackling the torque. These let the helicopter fly and hover with no trouble!

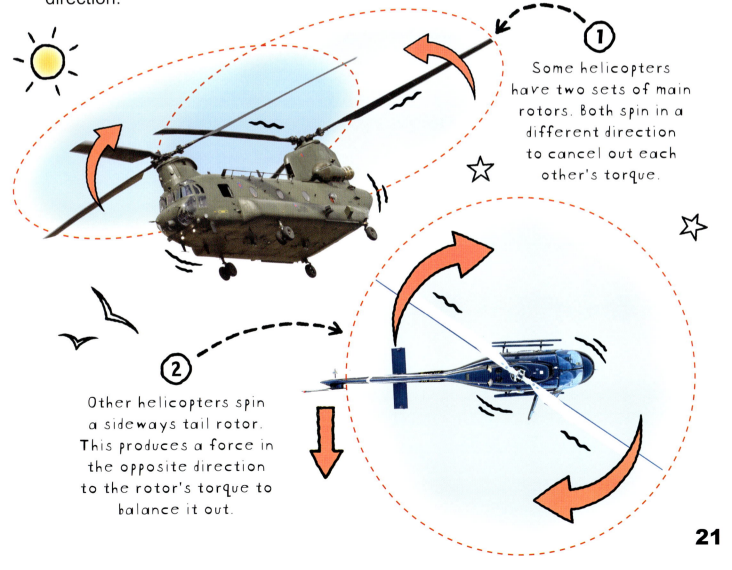

① Some helicopters have two sets of main rotors. Both spin in a different direction to cancel out each other's torque.

② Other helicopters spin a sideways tail rotor. This produces a force in the opposite direction to the rotor's torque to balance it out.

Why is petrol a problem?

Petrol, diesel and other fuels made from oil, power most of the planet's vehicles. They burn easily and fiercely to provide a powerful source of energy.

Explosive engine

Your family car, if fuelled by petrol, moves due to thousands of small explosions inside its internal combustion engine every minute.

Car engines usually have two, four or more cylinders where all the action occurs.

Petrol is sprayed into an engine cylinder where it is joined by air.

A rod called a piston moves into the cylinder to squeeze the fuel and air together.

A spark plug produces a spark which ignites the fuel and air, causing them to burn.

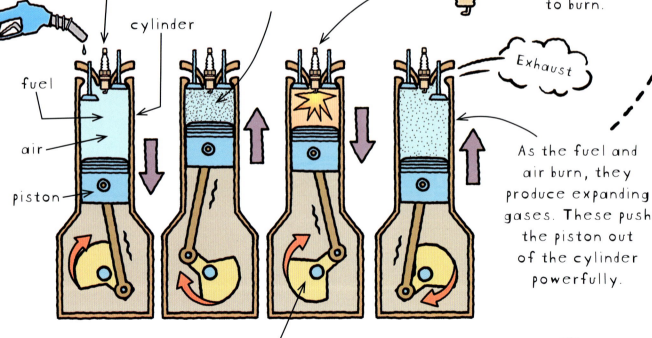

cylinder

fuel

air

piston

Exhaust

As the fuel and air burn, they produce expanding gases. These push the piston out of the cylinder powerfully.

A crank turns the up and down movement of the piston into a turning movement that spins the vehicle's wheels.

VROOM!
VROOOM!

Pollution problem

The gases from the engine cylinders eventually leave the car via exhaust pipes. Some of these gases are harmful to breathe in, while others are greenhouse gases which contribute to climate change.

Every year, a typical car releases about 4.6 tonnes of carbon dioxide – a key greenhouse gas. That's about the weight of two rhinos!

And there are more than a billion fossil fuel-burning cars, trucks, vans, buses and motorbikes on the world's roads. So, you can see how big the problem is.

Greenhouse gases

Certain gases such as carbon dioxide and nitrogen oxides in Earth's atmosphere trap the Sun's energy and reflect it back to Earth.

This helps warm the planet.

Atmosphere

PHEW, I NEED A COLD DRINK!

Over the past 150 years, industry and transport has pumped lots more greenhouse gases into the atmosphere.

They're now trapping extra heat, warming the planet even more and leading to climate change.

Solutions?

Plenty, starting with using cars less and walking, cycling and using public transport more. Electric vehicles can help, too. They use electricity instead of burning petrol.

23

How do you stop a speeding car?

A car racing along the road has a lot of energy and weight. So, when it's travelling at 90 or 100 km/h, it's going to take a lot of stopping. Amazingly, pads and discs, often smaller than a dinner plate, do all the hard work.

THANK GOODNESS OUR BRAKES WORK WELL!

EEEK!

Disc brakes

Metal discs called rotors are attached to each of a car's wheels. When a driver wants to slow down, they press the brake pedal. This forces liquid called brake fluid along tubes.

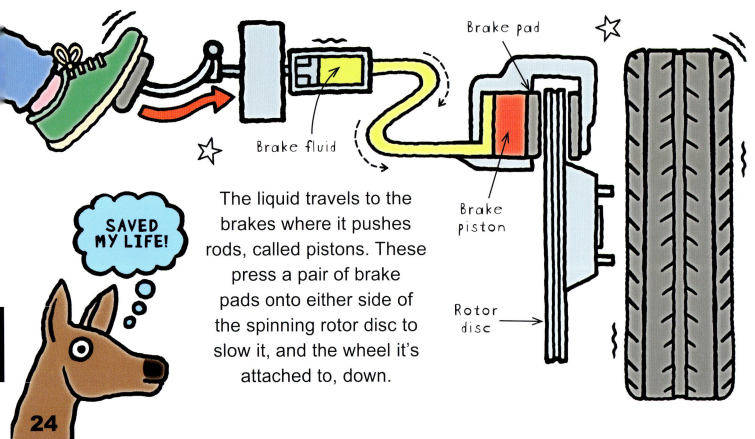

Brake pad

Brake fluid

Brake piston

Rotor disc

SAVED MY LIFE!

The liquid travels to the brakes where it pushes rods, called pistons. These press a pair of brake pads onto either side of the spinning rotor disc to slow it, and the wheel it's attached to, down.

Feeling friction

Brake pads in contact with the discs generate a lot of friction*. Most of the time, cars try to avoid friction as it slows their moving parts down and causes wear. With brakes, though, friction is positively encouraged!

* The force which occurs when two objects rub or slide across each other.

Hot stuff

Apart from slowing things down, friction also creates heat. You can feel this when you rub your hands together vigorously. Sometimes the friction created when a fast car brakes causes so much heat that the wheels smoke!

Balloon brakes

Top Fuel Dragsters are the fastest cars of all. They can reach speeds of over 500 km/h as they cross the finish line.

Brakes and pads can only generate so much stopping power, so dragsters use parachutes instead. These are released behind the car, catch the air and create lots of drag to slow the dragster down quickly.

How long can a submarine stay underwater?

WHAT'S THAT?

THAT'S THE SUN!

Submarines have the amazing ability to go deep underwater. Smaller subs can stay underwater for days, but big military submarines can manage three or four months at a time.

Going down

To get underwater in the first place, submarines are built with enormous ballast tanks. These can be filled with air or water to adjust the sub's weight. As a result, the submarine can dive down or rise upwards.

Down ... Air is forced out of ballast tanks and seawater floods in.

Sub becomes much heavier, denser than water and sinks.

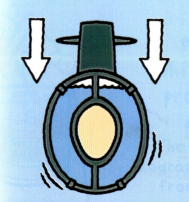

... And up again Water is flushed out of tanks which are filled with air.

The submarine becomes lighter than water and rises upwards towards the surface.

On the level

If the submarine fills its ballast tanks with the correct amounts of air and water, it can balance out its weight. Then, it neither falls nor rises and can cruise along underwater at a set depth.

Tall periscope gives view above the surface while the sub lurks below

Hinged flap called rudder is turned to steer the sub left or right

Escape hatch

Life underwater

The biggest submarines are longer than 1 ½ football pitches and carry 120-160 crew. All those people need to be fed and watered. So, large amounts of food is stored for each voyage.

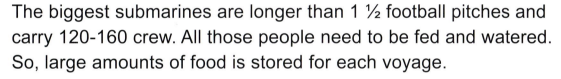

Desalination plants on board the sub remove the salt from seawater to create fresh water that can be drunk, cooked and washed with.

Life aboard a sub is cramped with only a tiny bunk to call your own. The Russian Typhoon class submarines, though, have a gym, sauna and a swimming pool!

CHEERS!

REALLY? A SWIMMING POOL? CAN I COME?

Quick-fire questions

Do pilots sleep?

Yes, but rarely while flying. If they do need a break or nap, an automated system called the autopilot keeps the plane on track or a second human pilot, the co-pilot, takes the controls. Some very long distance airliners, like the Boeing 787-9, have hidden compartments in the roof of their fuselage which contain beds for pilots and other aircrew to take a well-earned rest.

I HOPE THAT'S NOT THE PILOT SLEEPING

ZZZZZZz

What's the fastest-ever ship or boat?

The *Spirit of Australia* was an incredibly speedy motorboat built in Australian Ken Warby's back garden. In 1977, it set the world water speed record of 511 km/h. Warby's rapid record still stands today!

How do trains get their electricity?

Many electric trains get their electricity from overhead power wires. A spring-loaded arm called a pantograph makes contact with the wires. It carries electricity from the wires into the train's power car where it drives motors to turn the train's wheels.

Pantograph

Power car

In places where overhead electric cables aren't possible, electric trains use a third rail. This runs alongside the railway track and carries high-voltage electricity – never go near one! Metal blocks contact this rail and conduct electricity, carrying it to the train's power car.

How do giant ships dock at ports?

Some big ships are towed into place by small, but powerful, tugboats. Others use thrusters fitted near the front and back of their hull. When both the front and rear thrusters squirt water out together, they push the ship gently sideways. When thrusters at just one end operate, they push the front or rear of the ship, turning it round slowly.

I'M FEELING DIZZY!

Thrusters

Glossary

Accelerate To speed up and go faster.

Aerodynamics The study of the way air moves around things such as planes, trains and motor vehicles.

Atmosphere The blanket of gases that surround Earth.

Aviation relating to flight or air travel

Climate change The gradual change of Earth's weather patterns, mostly caused by the effects of greenhouse gases.

Density How heavy something is for its size.

Downforce A force that pushes some vehicles towards the ground when air flows over the vehicle.

Drag A force that slows down a moving object when air pushes against it.

Friction A force generated by two objects rubbing together that slows movement down and creates heat and wear.

Fuel A substance or material that is burned to produce heat or power.

Fuselage The body of an aircraft.

Gear Wheels with teeth which are used in cars, bikes and other vehicles to change the amount of speed or force with which parts of a machine turn.

Greenhouse gas A gas such as methane or carbon dioxide that helps trap heat in the atmosphere warming the planet and partially responsible for climate change.

Hull The main body of a ship.

Internal combustion engine A type of engine which burns fuel and air inside to produce power.

LiDAR Short for Light Detection and Ranging, this is a sensor system that sends out pulses of laser light to measure distances to objects.

Piston A rod that moves up and down a cylinder in, for example, an engine cylinder.

Power car The vehicle that pulls a train's carriages along the track.

Rudder A flap on the rear edge of an airplane's tail that controls whether a plane's nose points left or right.

Satnav Short for satellite navigation, these are electronic mapping systems that use signals from orbiting space satellites to provide accurate navigation for vehicles.

Sensor A device that collects information about a machine and its surroundings.

Streamlined When a vehicle or another object is shaped so that air flows easily over and around it.

Thrust A force that propels a vehicle forward.

Tonne A measure of weight equal to 1,000 kilograms.

Torque A turning or twisting force

Wind tunnels Tubes in which engineers generate strong winds to check how their machines will move through air.

Further reading

Websites

www.wondrium.com/the-science-of-flight
An in-depth series of videos about how aircraft fly.

afdc.energy.gov/vehicles/how-do-all-electric-cars-work
Compare how all-electric vehicles work with hybrid and petrol cars.

interestingengineering.com/how-do-self-driving-cars-work
Learn more about how driverless cars operate.

animagraffs.com/inside-a-jet-engine/
Travel inside a jet engine at this animated website to learn how engines generate huge power.

Books

Adventures In STEAM: Vehicles
by Georgia Amson-Bradshaw (Wayland, 2019)

How Ships Work
by Clive Gifford (Lonely Planet, 2020)

Awesome Engineering: Trains, Ships and Planes
by Sally Spray (Franklin Watts, 2019)

Infographic: How It Works: Machines and Motors
by Jon Richards (Wayland, 2019)

Kid Engineer: Working with Transport
by Sonya Newland (Wayland, 2021)

Index

A Question of Technology titles:

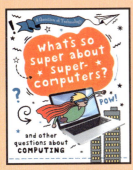

978 1 5263 2000 1 HB
978 1 5263 2001 8 PB

What is a computer?
What did the first computer look like?
Who was the first coder?
Why were early computers so BIG?
Why make microchips so tiny?
Where does all my data go?
Why do computers take
soooo long to start?
How does what I type
reach the screen?
How do computer games
know the score?
Is a bug the same as a virus?
Could a laser printer destroy the world?
What's so super about
supercomputers?

978 1 5263 2012 4 HB
978 1 5263 2013 1 PB

What are electronics?
Why won't touchscreens work
with gloves on?
Why do some phone calls travel into space?
How do electric guitars rock out?
How can a metal cylinder
power electronics?
Why is it hard to hold up a cash machine?
How do round camera lenses take
rectangular photos?
How does a rock tell the time?
Do solar panels work when it's cloudy?
How do blind people use electronics
and technology?
How can we see at night?
How does my phone know who I am?

978 1 5263 2008 7 HB
978 1 5263 2009 4 PB

What's the Internet?
Are the World Wide Web and
the Internet the same thing?
What was the first thing
sent over the Internet?
Can wind blow away WiFi?
Is the Web really full of spiders?
Is there one big Internet superhighway?
Why does the Internet need walls?
Why is TimBL an HTML hero?
Do I need wellies to go streaming?
Can you break the Internet?
What's the Internet of Things?
What's the digital divide?

978 1 5263 2006 3 HB
978 1 5263 2007 0 PB

What is an invention?
Who invented inventing?
How do inventors invent?
Do inventors make squillions?
What was the great telephone race?
Who invented the concrete piano?
Where are all the female inventors?
Were can openers really invented
50 years after cans?
Are inventions ever recycled?
How can a vest stop
speeding bullets?
How did a bird build a bullet train?
Do inventions ever occur
by accident?

978 1 5263 2011 7 HB
978 1 5263 2010 0 PB

What are machines?
How can air smash concrete?
How can light slice through steel?
How do fridges stay chilled?
How do microwave ovens cook
food without getting hot?
Why don't big cranes topple over?
What's the biggest digger?
How can machines see inside me?
How can machines keep
your heart going?
Can you 3D print a 3D printer?
How does a gale power
my games console?
How can we make machines
more green?

978 1 5263 2003 2 HB
978 1 5263 2002 5 PB

What is a robot?
What was the first robot?
How do robots know where to go?
Why do robots get all the boring jobs?
How do robots save lives?
Why are some robots astronauts?
Will robots take all our jobs?
Why don't more robots look like us?
Does a robot know it's holding a banana?
How small can robots go?
Can robots save the planet?
Will robots take over the world?

978 1 5263 2004 9 HB
978 1 5263 2005 6 PB

What is space?
Why can't we just fly to the Moon?
Why do things orbit?
How do space probes land?
Why haven't we explored
other galaxies?
Why send telescopes into space?
Do astronauts really grow in space?
What's for dinner in space?
How do you go to the toilet
in space?
Why do astronauts suit up
for spacewalks?
Are there aliens in space?
Will we ever live on Mars?

978 1 5263 1994 4 HB
978 1 5263 2995 1 PB

Transport tech
Can a driverless car get lost?
How does a plane turn left?
Why doesn't a 200,000-tonne
ship sink?
How do gears make
my bike super speedy?
Could an F1 car drive
upside-down on a ceiling?
Why do my ears pop when I'm flying?
Are crash test dummies
actually really smart?
How do helicopters stay up?
Why is petrol a problem?
How do you stop a speeding car?
How long can a submarine
stay underwater?